C000003198

WARWICKSHIRE
COUNTRY RECIPES

COMPILED BY
PIPPA GOMAR

ЯR
RAVETTE BOOKS

Published by Ravette Books Limited
3 Glenside Estate, Star Road
Partridge Green, Horsham,
Sussex RH13 8RA
(0403) 710392

Copyright in this collection © Pippa Gomar 1988
All rights reserved, including the right
of reproduction in whole or in part
in any form.

Production: Oval Projects Ltd.
Cover design: Jim Wire
Typesetting: Repro-type
Printing & binding: Nørhaven A/S

All recipes are given in Imperial and Metric
weights and measures. Where measurements
are given in 'cups', these are American cups,
holding 8 fluid ounces.

The recipes contained in this book are traditional
and many have been compiled from archival sources.
Every effort has been made to ensure that the recipes
are correct.

RECITES

SAVOURIES

PUDDINGS

CAKES and BREAD

SUNDRIES

PRESERVES and PICKLES

WARWICKSHIRE

Warwickshire is a beautiful, mainly rural county that has inspired many poets and writers, particularly William Shakespeare, born in Stratford upon Avon and George Eliot, born in Nuneaton, to extol the glories of the countryside. 'That shire which we the heart of England well may call' (Michael Drayton — poet) contains the centre of England in the village of Minworth, although there are several places in the county that lay claim to this title.

Warwickshire was once largely covered by the vast Forest of Arden. It still boasts some of the finest woodlands in England, providing fine hunting for the nobility and plentiful meat for their feasts.

Warwick Castle was built in the 14th century as a fortification and was converted to a mansion in the 17th century. There was much fine banqueting during both periods, using local produce — including fish from the river Avon which the Castle overlooks. Both trout and coarse fishing are carried on in the county's waterways — in its rivers and canals, including the Grand Union Canal in Warwick.

The network of man-made canals constructed in the 18th century, and still much in evidence today, once formed an important link with London, and played a vital part in the local diet. They were responsible not only for the transportation to London of produce and manufactured goods from the growing industrial towns of Warwickshire and the Midlands, but also for bringing a variety of foodstuffs from London back to Warwickshire for those who could afford to buy them. The wealthy lived on a variety of foods which included exotic fruits such as apricots, quince, figs, dates and also cocoa. In contrast, the diet of the ordinary country folk relied on produce from the land. Hunting, shooting and fishing were more a necessity for survival than for sport. Most cottagers kept a pig for slaughter and many kept chickens for their eggs. Pork was an important source of protein and this is reflected in the numerous recipes (such as Jellied Chitterlings and Pig's Pudding) made with pork or some part of the pig as the main ingredient.

The county has good pastureland which supports herds of sheep and cattle. In the 18th century there were a great many dairy cows which provided especially creamy milk used for cheesemaking. The cheese had a good reputation at that time and was apparently similar to Gloucester cheese as we know it today. It is now no longer made, but diary farming continues, and market gardens and orchards flourish.

Beer was another great staple. Many kinds were brewed in the county, each with its own name. At Ilmington, 'Black Strap', 'Ruffle-me-Cap', 'Fine and Clear' and 'Table Beer' were brewed; and among those from Alderminster were 'Twine in the Belly', 'Twice as Many' and 'Tip Tap'. There was even a beer especially for children called 'Tilly Willy'. Brewing occured mainly in March and October from the barley grown in the county. Many households brewed their own beer and would invite their neighbours to join them in sampling the final product. Cider, stout, mulled ale and wine using flowers and fruit from the hedgerows were also made, and each had to be drunk from the correct vessel. Beer was drunk from a pewter tankard, stout from a china mug and cider from a horn cup.

Customs and superstitions are often associated with those basic foods which were important to country folk. Apples were thought to cause a bad stomach-ache if eaten before St. Swithins Day (15th July). Bread was often marked with a cross to protect it from witchcraft and it was believed that a teaspoon of rain collected on Ascension Day would prevent the bread from being too heavy if added to the dough.

Other customs are associated with the farming year, which began on Plough Monday (the first Monday after 6th January) with a meal at which Plum Pudding was one of the main items. The beginning of the lambing season was announced by the birth of the first lamb and the farmer was rewarded with a large thick pancake. Stuffed Chine of Pork was served at the Sheep Shearing Supper, an important occasion mentioned by Shakespeare in *The Winter's Tale*. It is encouraging that some of these country customs are still recognised and practised in Warwickshire today.

'Our Warwickshire the heart of England is,
As you must evidently have prov'd by this:
Having it with more spirit dignified,
Than all our English Counties are beside'.

Sir Aston Cokain (1658)

RABBIT BROTH

2 rabbit legs
4 oz (100 g) stewing steak
3 pints (1.75 litres/ 8 cups) water
A little salt and pepper
1 onion
1 small turnip
1 bay leaf
3 tablespoons chopped fresh parsley

Cut the rabbit meat and the stewing steak into small pieces.

Put into a large saucepan with the water, salt and pepper.

Bring to the boil.

Skim any scum from the surface.

Chop the onion and turnip and add them to the soup.

Add the bay leaf and the chopped parsley.

Bring to the boil again and simmer gently for 3 hours.

Strain, and leave to cool.

When cool skim off any excess fat.

Re-heat before serving and serve garnished with fresh parsley.

GREEN PEA SOUP

This soup has been a favourite since the Middle Ages.

1 lettuce
1 cucumber
1 lb (450 g) fresh or frozen garden peas
1 clove of garlic, crushed
3 oz (75 g) butter
2 pints (1.15 litres/ 5 cups) ham stock
A little parsley
A pinch of mace
2 oz (50 g) bacon
A little salt and pepper

Chop the lettuce and slice the cucumber finely.

Put the peas, lettuce, cucumber and crushed garlic clove into a saucepan with the butter.

Gently cook the vegetables until soft.

Finely chop the parsley, leaving some unchopped for a garnish.

Add the stock, parsley and mace.

Chop the bacon and add to the soup.

Bring to the boil and simmer, covered, for 30 minutes.

Liquidize the soup or rub the ingredients through a wire-mesh sieve.

Season with salt and pepper and re-heat.

Serve garnished with parsley.

CARROT SOUP

2 onions
2 oz (50 g) butter
1 lb (450 g) carrots
1 small turnip
4 sticks of celery
A large slice of ham
A little parsley
2 pints (1.15 litres/ 5 cups) beef or mutton stock
A pinch of salt and pepper

Chop the onions and cook gently in the butter until soft.

Chop the carrots, turnips and celery and add to the pan.

Cook gently for a few minutes.

Chop the ham and parsley.

Add the stock, ham, chopped parsley, and the salt and pepper.

Bring to the boil and simmer for about 40 minutes or until the vegetables are completely tender.

Liquidize the soup or rub through a wire-mesh sieve.

Serve garnished with parsley and a swirl of cream.

VEGETABLE MARROW SOUP

Serves 6

By the beginning of the 19th century almost every kitchen garden grew marrows on a manure heap. Cottagers grew them outside their pig sties.

1 onion
1 large marrow
2 oz (50 g) flour
2 oz (50 g) butter
1 pint (600 ml/ 2½ cups) milk
2 pints (1.15 litres/ 5 cups) white stock
A little salt and pepper

Finely chop the onion.

Peel the marrow and slice it in half length-ways.

Scoop out the seeds and cut the marrow flesh into cubes.

Gently cook the onion and marrow in the butter for 15 to 20 minutes.

Add the flour and cook for a few minutes.

Add the milk and stock and simmer until the marrow is tender.

Liquidize the ingredients or rub through a wire-mesh sieve.

Season with salt and pepper.

Return to a gentle heat until hot again.

STEWED CARP

Although Warwickshire is a land-locked county, fresh water fish are found in its rivers and man-made canals.

2½ lbs (1.25 kg) carp
A little salt
¼ pint (150 ml/ ⅔ cup) dry white wine
¾ pint (450 ml/ 2 cups) water
1 onion
A bouquet garni
1 oz (25 g) butter
1 teaspoon anchovy essence

Scale and gut the carp. Rub the cavity with salt.

Soak the fish in salted water for a few hours.

Drain and put the carp in a large saucepan or fish kettle.

Add the wine and water.

Slice the onion and sprinkle over the carp.

Add the bouquet garni.

Bring to the boil and simmer for 20-30 minutes or until the fish is tender.

Remove the fish, reserving the stock, and keep it warm on a serving dish.

In a saucepan melt the butter until it browns.

Gradually add about ¼ pint (150 ml/ ⅔ cup) of the fish stock.

Add the anchovy essence and heat until the sauce has thickened.

Pour the sauce over the carp and serve.

CRAYFISH AND BACON SAVOURY   Serves 4

8 oz (225 g) bacon rashers
8 crayfish tails
A little salt and pepper
4 slices of bread
1 oz (25 g) butter

Grill the bacon rashers and chop into small pieces.

Remove the meat from the crayfish tails and chop into small pieces.

Mix the bacon and crayfish and season with a little salt and pepper.

Cook for a few minutes in the butter.

Toast the bread on both sides and butter one side.

Spread the crayfish and bacon mixture over the toast and serve immediately.

CHICKEN FRICASSEY

Serves 4

This is one of the very few recipes for old chickens, from the time when chickens were kept for their eggs and only eaten when they were past egg-laying age.

4 chicken pieces
Water
A pinch of salt and pepper
A bouquet garni
1 oz (25 g) butter
1 oz (25 g) flour
½ pint (300 ml/ 1¼ cups) single cream
¼ pint (150 ml/ ⅔ cup) dry white wine
2 egg yolks
8 oz (225 g) mushrooms
A pinch of grated nutmeg

Put the chicken into a large saucepan and cover with water.

Season with salt and pepper and add the bouquet garni.

Bring to the boil and simmer for about 45 minutes until the chicken pieces are tender.

Remove the chicken from the saucepan and reserve the stock.

Melt the butter and add the flour.

Cook for a few minutes then gradually add ½ pint (300 ml/ 1¼ cups) of the stock.

Stir in the cream and the wine.

Beat the egg yolks and stir them into the sauce.

Chop the mushrooms and add them to the pan.

Return the chicken pieces to the sauce and sprinkle with a pinch of grated nutmeg.

Heat gently until the sauce has thickened.

Serve immediately.

PARTRIDGE CASSEROLE

Serves 4

This is an 18th century recipe. It should be served with thick slices of bread. Partridge has a delicate flavour not unlike good chicken and casseroling is an excellent way of cooking birds at the end of the season.

2 partridges, hung, plucked and drawn
4 small onions
12 oz (350 g) carrots
1 bay leaf
4 oz (100 g) lean bacon
A pinch of salt and pepper
A pinch of dried parsley
A pinch of dried thyme
4 rashers of streaky bacon
1 Savoy cabbage
1½ pints (900 ml/ 3¾ cups) stock made with the giblets
   from the partridges

To make the stock:

Put all the giblets into a small saucepan.

Add a slice of onion and carrot, the bay leaf and a little salt and pepper.

Bring to the boil, cover, and simmer for 30 minutes.

Cool and strain.

To make the casserole:

Slice two of the onions and all the carrots.

Dice the lean bacon.

Put the onions, carrots and diced bacon into a casserole dish.

Season with salt, pepper, parsley and thyme.

Peel the remaining two onions but leave whole.

Place one onion into the cavity of each partridge.

Truss the birds with a skewer and string.

Wrap two bacon rashers over each bird.

Place the birds on the bed of vegetables and bacon in the casserole dish.

Parboil the cabbage for about 3 minutes.

Drain and cut into quarters.

Pack the cabbage around the partridges in the casserole dish.

Pour the stock over.

Cook in a moderate oven for 2 hours.

Oven: 325°F/160°C Gas Mark 3

RABBIT PIE

1 rabbit, jointed
8 oz (225 g) bacon
2 onions
8 oz (225 g) carrots
2 sticks of celery
A little salt and pepper
2 oz (50 g) butter
1 tablespoon chopped parsley
A little grated nutmeg
Stock or water to cover

For the pastry:
8 oz (225 g) flour
4 oz (100 g) butter
A pinch of salt
A little cold water to mix

Soak the rabbit joints in salted water for about 2 hours.

Drain and pat dry.

Chop the bacon into small pieces.

Chop the onions, carrots and the celery.

Put the vegetables into a saucepan with the butter, cooking gently for a few minutes until the onion is soft.

Put the vegetables in the bottom of a pie dish.

Arrange the rabbit joints and the bacon on top.

Sprinkle with salt, pepper, chopped parsley and grated nutmeg.

Add enough stock or water to cover the ingredients.

To make the pastry:

Sift the flour and salt.

Rub in the butter until the mixture resembles breadcrumbs.

Add enough cold water to make a soft dough.

Put to one side for 30 minutes.

Roll out the pastry and cover the pie dish, sealing securely by moistening the edges.

Bake for 25 minutes at a high temperature.

Reduce the temperature and continue cooking for one hour.

Serve hot or cold.

Oven: 425°F/220°C Gas Mark 7
Reduce to: 350°F/180°C Gas Mark 4

JUGGED HARE WITH
FORCEMEAT BALLS

Serves 6

This dish would originally have been cooked in a tall eartenware jug, hence the name.

1 jointed hare
2 oz (50 g) flour
A little salt and pepper
2 oz (50 g) butter
2 onions
¼ pint (150 ml/ ⅔ cup) red wine
2 tablespoons redcurrant jelly

For the forcemeat balls:
Liver from the hare
2 rashers of streaky bacon
4 oz (100 g) shredded suet
6 oz (175 g) fresh breadcrumbs
1 teaspoon mixed dried herbs
Grated rind of ½ a lemon
A few sprigs of parsley
A little salt and pepper
2 eggs

Remove the meat from the bones of the hare.

Put the bones into a saucepan and cover with water.

Bring to the boil, cover and simmer for 1-1½ hours.

Season the flour with salt and pepper.

Toss the meat in the flour and fry in the butter until brown.

Put the meat in a large casserole dish.

Chop the onions and fry in the remaining butter.

Add to the casserole.

Add any remaining flour to the butter and juices in the pan and cook for a few minutes.

Gradually add about ½ pint (300 ml/ 1¼ cups) of the stock prepared from the bones and stir until slightly thickened.

Stir in the wine and redcurrant jelly.

Pour the liquid over the meat in the casserole.

Cover and cook in a moderate oven for 2½ hours.

To make the forcemeat balls:

Mince the liver and bacon.

Add the suet, breadcrumbs, mixed dried herbs and lemon rind.

Chop the parsley and add it to the mixture.

Season with a little salt and pepper.

Mix the ingredients together well.

Beat the eggs and add to the mixture until it has a firm consistency.

Make small balls with the mixture and put into a greased ovenproof dish.

Bake for 30 minutes with the hare, basting and turning occasionally.

Serve the hare with the forcemeat balls.

Oven: 325°F/160°C Gas Mark 3

VENISON ROLL

The roll was originally tied in a cloth and boiled but baking in the oven is easier and makes an equally tasty dish. Lamb may be used instead of venison. It is alleged that William Shakespeare was once caught poaching deer in Charlecote Park and was punished for it.

1½ lbs (675 g) venison
8 oz (225 g) bacon
6 oz (175 g) breadcrumbs
1 onion
2 tablespoons parsley
1 tablespoon fresh thyme
2 eggs
2 oz (50 g) flour
A little salt and pepper
Redcurrant jelly
Brown gravy

Mince the venison and bacon.

Chop the onion finely.

Mix the venison, bacon, onion and breadcrumbs.

Chop 1 tablespoon of the parsley and the thyme.

Add the chopped herbs to the mixture.

Beat the eggs and add to the mixture.

Shape into a long roll.

Season the flour with salt and pepper.

Coat the roll with the flour.

Wrap tightly in foil and place in a casserole dish.

Put on enough boiling water to cover the role.

Bake gently for 2 hours.

15 minutes before serving remove the roll from the water, take off the foil and place on an ovenproof serving dish.

Return it to the oven to dry and brown.

Garnish with the remaining parsley and serve with redcurrant jelly and gravy.

Oven: 300°F/150°C Gas Mark 2

MUTTON COLLOPS

This dish is known to have been eaten in Stratford upon Avon in 1820. Lamb may be used instead of mutton.

1 lb (450 g) chump end of mutton or lamb, minced
1 oz (25 g) flour
1 onion
1 tablespoon mushroom ketchup
2 tablespoons Worcestershire sauce
A pinch of cayenne pepper
A little salt and pepper
Grated rind of ½ a lemon
½ pint (300 ml/ 1¼ cups) stock
1½ lbs (675 g) potatoes

Chop the onion.

Mix the meat, onion and flour in a large saucepan.

Add the mushroom ketchup, Worcestershire sauce, cayenne pepper, salt, pepper, grated lemon rind and stock.

Bring to the boil and simmer for 1 hour.

Boil the potatoes for 15 to 20 minutes until soft.

Mash the potatoes and pipe or spoon them around the edge of a serving dish while still hot.

Turn the meat mixture into the centre and serve immediately.

MUTTON CHOPS
WITH CHESTNUTS

Serves 6

Pork chops may also be used for this recipe.

6 mutton or lamb loin chops
1 oz (25 g) flour
A little salt and pepper
2 oz (50 g) lard or dripping
2 onions
½ pint (300 ml/ 1¼ cups) stock
¼ pint (150 ml/ ⅔ cup) red wine
12 oz (350 g) boiled and peeled chestnuts
A pinch of dried thyme

Trim the fat from the chops.

Season with salt and pepper.

Coat the chops with the seasoned flour and fry in the lard
or dripping until brown on all sides.

Place in a casserole dish.

Chop the onions and fry in the remaining fat in the pan.

Scatter the onions over the chops.

Add the chestnuts.

Pour the stock and wine over the chops and chestnuts.

Season with the thyme.

Cover and bake for 1½ hours.

Serve with boiled potatoes and a salad.

Oven: 325°F/160°C Gas Mark 3

STEWED LAMBS' KIDNEYS

Serves 6

18 lambs' kidneys
3 onions
4 cooking apples
2 pints (1.15 litres/ 5 cups) stock
1 bouquet garni
A little salt and pepper
2 tablespoons cornflour
2 tablespoons flour
2 oz (50 g) butter

Skin the kidneys and remove the cores.

Season the flour with salt and pepper.

Coat the kidneys in the seasoned flour.

Melt the butter in a pan.

Add the kidneys and brown on all sides.

Transfer the kidneys to a casserole dish.

Slice the onions and fry in the remaining butter until soft.

Peel, core and slice the apples.

Transfer the onions and apples to the casserole dish.

Pour the stock over and add the bouquet garni.

Cook very gently for 4 hours.

Just before serving, thicken the stock with the cornflour dissolved in a little water.

Serve with triangular croûtons.

Oven: 275°F/140°C Gas Mark 1

STEAK AND KIDNEY PIE

Serves 6

1½ lbs (675 g) rump steak
12 oz (350 g) kidney
1 oz (25 g) flour
1 onion
2 oz (50 g) butter
A little salt and pepper
¾ pint (450 ml/ 2 cups) brown stock
¼ pint (150 ml/ ⅔ cup) red wine
1 bay leaf
1 tablespoon tomato purrée
8 oz (225 g) puff pastry

Chop the onion and fry in the butter until soft.

Cut the steak and kidney into 1 inch (2.5 cm) cubes.

Season the flour with a little salt and pepper.

Toss the steak and kidney in the seasoned flour.

Brown on all sides in the remaining butter in the pan.

Put the steak, kidney and onion into a 2 pint (1.15 litre/ 5 cups) pie dish.

Stir the remaining flour into the remaining butter and cook for a few minutes. Gradually add the stock and wine.

Pour into the pie dish until it almost covers the meat.

Add the bay leaf and the tomato purée.

Cover the dish with foil and bake gently for 1½ hours.

Remove from the oven and remove the foil.

Roll out the pastry and cover the pie dish, moistening the edges to seal.

Bake at a higher temperature for 25 minutes.

Oven: 300°F/150°C Gas Mark 2
Increase to: 425°F/220°C Gas Mark 7

PAIL DINNER

Warwickshire has many canals, including the famous Grand Union Canal and the Stratford upon Avon Canal. Cooking facilities have always been rather limited on the narrow canal boats. This old recipe is for a complete dinner cooked in a large pail over a small flame. The meal would take all morning to cook. When it was ready the layers of apples and the top suet crust layer were removed and kept hot, while the broth, meat, vegetables and potatoes were eaten.

For the suet crust pastry:
8 oz (225 g) self-raising flour
4 oz (100 g) suet
A pinch of salt
About ¼ pint (150 ml/ ⅔ cup) water

For the meat filling:
1½ lbs (675 g) stewing steak
2 onions
4 carrots
2 small turnips
Stock to cover
1½ lbs (675 g) potatoes

For the sweet filling:
1½ lbs (675 g) cooking apples
2 oz (50 g) butter
1 oz (25 g) caster sugar

To make the meat filling:

Chop the meat into cubes.

Slice the onions, carrots and turnips.

Fill the bottom of an earthenware jar with layers of meat, onions, carrots and turnips.

Pour in just enough stock to cover the ingredients.

To make the suet crust pastry:

Sift the flour and salt.

Stir in the suet.

Gradually add enough cold water to make a soft dough.

Divide the dough into two.

Roll out one half and cover the meat, onion, carrots and turnips.

Put the earthenware jar into a pail containing water to come half way up the sides of the jar.

Bring to the boil and simmer gently for 2 hours.

Remove from the heat.

Slice the potatoes and place on top of the suet crust.

Roll out the remaining dough and place on top of the potatoes.

To make the sweet filling:

Peel, core and slice the apples and place them on top of the suet crust.

Sprinkle with sugar.

Cut the butter into small pieces and place on top of the apples.

Cover the jar with a buttered cloth or foil.

Return to the heat and simmer for a further 2 hours.

WARWICKSHIRE PORK PIE

For the pastry:
1 lb (450 g) flour
A pinch of salt
8 oz (225 g) lard
¼ pint (150 ml/ ⅔ cup) water and milk combined

For the filling:
3 lbs (1.5 kg) pork
A little salt and pepper
A pinch of cayenne pepper
2 tablespoons water
1 egg white

To make the pastry:

Sift the flour and salt together.

Rub half the lard into the flour.

Put the remaining lard into a saucepan with the milk and water.

Bring to the boil then gradually add to the flour.

Stir well then knead until smooth.

The pastry must be raised while it is still warm, as follows:

Roll out ¾ of the pastry dough into a large circular shape about ½ inch (1 cm) thick.

Gently mould it around a floured and greased round pot or cake tin.

Turn the pot or tin onto its side and roll it a few times to smooth the outsides and loosen the pastry.

Leave the pastry on the pot or tin for 15 minutes or until cool.

Remove the pastry case from the pot or tin.

To make the filling:

Cut the pork into small cubes.

Sprinkle with salt, pepper and cayenne pepper.

Pack the meat into the pie crust.

Add the water.

Roll out the remaining pastry dough and cover the contents of the pie, moistening and pinching the edges to seal.

Brush with egg white to glaze.

Cook on a low heat for 2½-3 hours.

Oven: 300°F/150°C Gas Mark 2

WARWICK PIG'S PUDDING

Makes 8 large

This is a local variation of black pudding. An old superstition had it that if an old wig belonging to a clergyman was hung in the chimney above the cooking range, it would prevent the puddings bursting during cooking.

1 lb (450 g) groats (dried oats stripped of their husks)
Water
8 oz (225 g) breadcrumbs
1 leek
A pinch of sage
A pinch of thyme
1 oz (25 g) salt
1 tablespoon black pepper
1 pint (600 ml/ 2½ cups) pig's blood
12 oz (350 g) lean pork
1 lb (450 g) pork fat
Sausage skins (obtainable from butchers)

Put the groats in a large saucepan with four times their volume of water.

Bring to the boil and simmer for 30 minutes or until the groats are soft.

Mix in the breadcrumbs.

Chop the leek and add to the mixture.

Add the sage, thyme, salt and pepper.

Dice the pork and pork fat and add to the mixture.

Add the pig's blood and mix well.

Put the mixture into the sausage skins and tie loosely.

Drop the sausages into hot but not boiling water and boil for 20 minutes or until the blood comes out when the puddings are pricked with a needle.

To serve, heat the puddings in hot water for about 10 minutes or cut into rounds and grill or fry.

Serve for breakfast with a mixed grill.

Alternatively the pudding mixture may be turned into a grease baking tin and baked in the oven for 45 minutes.

Oven: 350°F/180°C Gas Mark 4

JELLIED CHITTERLING

The chitterlings are the intestines and other parts of the pig's entrails. Occasionally jellied chitterlings can be found cooked and pressed like tongue in delicatessens.

1 lb (450 g) pig's heart, intestines, liver and sweet bread
A little salt and pepper
1 tablespoon fresh sage
1 oz (25 g) aspic

Put the pig's fry into a saucepan and cover with water.

Season with salt and pepper.

Add the sage.

Bring to the boil and simmer gently for 1 hour.

Remove the pig's fry from the pan.

Chop finely and put into a greased mould.

Strain the stock and boil rapidly to reduce to ¾ pint (450 ml/ 2 cups).

Mix the aspic with a little of the stock and add to the remaining stock.

Pour over the meat and leave to set.

Turn out and serve garnished with sage.

FAGGOTS

Serves 4

Traditionally, faggots are cooked in small squares of pig's caul which is part of the animal's stomach (available from butchers). Balls of the mixture are wrapped in the caul squares and are then put into a roasting tin with the joins underneath.

1 lb (450 g) pig's liver
½ pint (300 ml/ 1¼ cups) milk
4 oz (100 g) fat pork
1 onion
2 eggs
A large pinch of grated nutmeg
A little salt and pepper
6 oz (175 g) breadcrumbs
Beef stock to mix
Pig's caul squares (optional)

Soak the liver in milk for at least an hour.

Mince the liver, pork and onion.

Beat the eggs and add the grated nutmeg, salt and pepper.

Stir into the liver mixture.

Work in the breadcrumbs to give a stiff consistency, adding a little stock if more liquid is required.

Press into a greased baking tin, or wrap in squares of pig's caul.

Cover with tin foil.

Bake for about 45 minutes until browned.

Oven: 375°F/190°C Gas Mark 5

STUFFED CHINE OF PORK

Serves 6

This dish is traditionally served on Mothering Sunday each year. It was also served at the sheep-shearing supper held at the beginning of June.

The Chine is the forequarter of pork without the leg.

5 lbs (2.25 kg) chine of pork
A handful of parsley
1 egg yolk
6 oz (175 g) fresh breadcrumbs
1 oz (25 g) butter

Put the pork into a large saucepan and cover with water.

Bring to the boil and simmer for 30 minutes.

Remove the meat from the saucepan and make several cuts in it.

Stuff sprigs of parsley into each slit with the stalk ends first.

Beat the egg yolk and brush the meat with it.

Cover with the breadcrumbs, pressing them firmly onto the meat.

Melt the butter and brush the meat all over.

Bake at a high temperature for 20 minutes.

Reduce the oven temperature and continue cooking for 3 hours.

Serve garnished with parsley sprigs and accompanied by spinach or broccoli.

Oven: 425°F/220°C Gas Mark 7
Reduce to: 325°F/160°C Gas Mark 3

RASTONS

For the majority of country people in the Middle Ages, pork or bacon was the only kind of meat eaten during the winter unless they were lucky enough to catch a pigeon or rabbit.

6 bread rolls
4 oz (100 g) butter
6 oz (175 g) bacon
4 oz (100 g) mushrooms
A little salt and pepper
3 oz (75 g) cheese

Cut the tops off the bread rolls.

Scoop out the insides and crumble to make breadcrumbs.

Melt 3 oz (75 g) of the butter and add the breadcrumbs.

Chop the bacon and fry with the breadcrumbs.

Wash and chop the mushrooms and add to the cooked mixture.

Season with salt and pepper and cook until the mushrooms are tender.

Pile the mixture into the bread roll cases.

Replace the lids and brush all over with the remaining melted butter.

Grate the cheese and sprinkle over the lids.

Bake in a moderately high oven for 10 minutes and serve hot.

Oven: 375°F/190°C Gas Mark 5

BACON JACK

This dish was taken as a midday meal to the farm workers after a morning's hay-making, wrapped in cloth to keep it hot. It probably acquired its name from the habit of cutting it into pieces with a 'jack' knife.

For the pastry:
12 oz (350 g) flour
A pinch of salt
6 oz (175 g) shredded suet
Cold water to mix

For the filling:
12 oz (350 g) boiled ham
2 onions
1 large potato
A pinch of mixed herbs
A pinch of salt and freshly ground black pepper

To make the pastry:

Sift the flour and salt together.

Add the suet and mix to a soft dough with cold water.

Roll out the pastry into a rectangle about 12 inches by 8 inches (30 cm by 20 cm).

To make the filling:

Chop the ham into small cubes.

Chop the onions and potato.

Spread the ham, onions and potato over the pastry dough.

Sprinkle with the mixed herbs, salt and pepper.

Roll up the dough from the long side like a Swiss-roll, moistening the edges with water to seal securely.

Wrap the roll in greaseproof paper and then either in a well buttered and floured pudding cloth or in tin foil.

Boil in a pan of water for 2 hours.

Transfer the roll to an ovenproof dish and place in a moderate oven for 10 minutes to dry out slightly.

Serve immediately.

Oven: 350°F/180°C Gas Mark 4

BRUMMY BACON CAKES

Serves 4

The colloquial name for a person who comes from Birmingham is 'Brummy'. The city was the greatest manufacturing centre of the Midlands being accessible by coach from London in the 18th century and by rail a century later.

4 oz (100 g) streaky bacon rashers
8 oz (225 g) self-raising flour
A pinch of salt
1 oz (25 g) butter
4 oz (100 g) cheese
¼ pint (150 ml/ ⅔ cup) milk
1 tablespoon tomato ketchup
A dash of Worcestershire sauce

Grill or fry the bacon until it is crisp.

Sift the flour and salt.

Rub in the butter.

Chop the bacon and add to the mixture.

Grate the cheese and add half to the flour and bacon mixture.

Stir in the tomato ketchup, Worcestershire sauce and enough milk to make a soft dough.

Roll out the dough to make an 8 inch (20 cm) circle.

Brush with milk and sprinkle with the remaining cheese.

Cut into 8 wedges and arrange on a greased baking sheet.

Bake in a fairly hot oven for 30 minutes.

Oven: 400°F/200°C Gas Mark 6

WELSH RAREBIT

4 tablespoons ale
8 oz (225 g) cheese
1 teaspoon made-up mustard
A little salt and pepper
2 oz (50 g) butter
4-8 slices of bread

Put the ale into a saucepan.

Grate the cheese and add to the ale.

Cook gently until the cheese has melted.

Stir in the mustard, butter, salt and pepper.

Heat gently.

Toast the bread on both sides and butter one side.

Pour the cheese mixture onto the middle of each slice of toast and allow to spread to the edges.

Brown the cheese mixture under the grill for a few minutes before serving.

HERB PANCAKES

A handful of parsley, thyme and chives.
2 oz (50 g) butter
8 oz (225 g) cooked ham
8 pancakes
¼ pint (150 ml/ ⅔ cup) stock

Chop the herbs finely.

Gently cook them in the butter for a few minutes.

Mince or finely chop the ham and stir into the herb and butter mixture.

Place a little of the herb and ham mixture onto each pancake and roll up.

Place the rolled up pancakes into a greased ovenproof dish side by side.

Pour in the stock.

Bake in a moderate oven for 30 minutes.

Serve hot.

Oven: 350°F/180°C Gas Mark 4

FRYING HERBS

Sorrel was popular several centuries ago. Spinach works as well for this recipe today.

1 lb (450 g) spinach or sorrel
1 lettuce
2 oz (50 g) spring onions
2 oz (50 g) parsley
3 oz (75 g) butter
A little salt and pepper
1 tablespoon lemon juice

Trim and wash the spinach or sorrel.

Remove the heart from the lettuce and discard the outer leaves.

Chop the onions, parsley, spinach or sorrel and lettuce heart.

Melt the butter in a frying pan and add the vegetables and herbs.

Season with a little salt and pepper.

Add the lemon juice.

Cover and cook for about 20 minutes or until the greens are tender.

Serve with liver, bacon or eggs.

PANCAKES

Tradition has it that on Shrove Tuesday the Pancake Bell was rung in Ilmington. This was a signal for the parish clerk to visit farms to collect pancakes in a large basket. As he called at the farms he would sing 'Link it, lank it, gi'e me a pankit'. It is not known whether the food was to give away to the poor, or to augment his own meagre stipend.

2 eggs
½ pint (300 ml/ 1¼ cups) single cream
1 oz (25 g) flour
4 oz (100 g) butter

Beat the eggs.

Stir in the cream and beat well.

Sift the flour over the mixture whisking all the time.

Melt the butter in a small saucepan and pour into the batter.

Stir well.

Leave for 30 minutes before making into pancakes.

Fry a little at a time in a frying pan. No extra butter or fat should be needed.

Keep the pancakes hot while the remainder are made.

WARWICKSHIRE PUDDING

Serves 4-6

4 oz (100 g) butter
3 oz (75 g) caster sugar
3 eggs
8 oz (225 g) flour
½ pint (300 ml/ 1¼ cups) milk
12 oz (350 g) raspberry jam

Cream the butter and sugar until pale and fluffy.

Gradually stir in the eggs and flour.

Add the milk to make a batter.

Grease a 2 pint (1.15 litres/ 5 cups) pudding basin.

Line the basin with 8 oz (225 g) of the jam.

Pour in the batter.

Cover with foil and tie down with string.

Put into a saucepan of boiling water.

Steam for 1½ hours.

Warm the remaining jam and serve the pudding with the extra jam poured over the top.

APRICOT FROISE

Recipes for similiar kinds of froise or frayse date back to the 15th century. They were often made with bacon, meat and vegetables instead of fruit.

For the batter:
8 oz (225 g) flour
A pinch of salt
4 oz (100 g) caster sugar
2 eggs
2 oz (50 g) butter
½ pint (300 ml/ 1¼ cups) milk
4 tablespoons double cream

For the filling:
1 lb (450 g) fresh apricots
2 oz (50 g) butter
1 oz (25 g) caster sugar

To make the batter:

Mix the flour, salt and sugar together.

Make a well in the middle of the bowl and break one egg into it, gradually working in the flour from the sides.

Separate the remaining egg and add the yolk to the mixture.

Stir the eggs in well.

Melt the butter and add, beating well.

Add the milk and cream and beat again.

Leave for 30 minutes.

Whisk the egg whites until stiff and fold into the batter.

To make the filling:

Blanch the apricots in boiling water for 1 minute and remove the skins while still warm.

Cut each apricot in half and remove the stones.

Melt the butter in a frying pan and fry the apricot halves for a few minutes.

Remove the fruit from the pan.

Pour in half of the batter.

Cook over a fairly high heat, and as the batter begins to set, spoon the apricot halves on top.

Sprinkle the sugar over the fruit.

Pour on the remaining batter.

When the bottom of the froise has browned, turn it over.

Add a little more butter and brown on the other side.

Serve immediately with cream.

APRICOT PIE

12 apricots
2 oz (50 g) caster sugar
4 egg yolks
2 egg whites
¼ pint (150 ml/ ⅔ cup) double cream
12 oz (350 g) puff pastry
Milk to glaze

For the puff pastry:
6 oz (175 g) plain flour
4 oz (100 g) butter
Salt
Water to mix
For a richer pastry use equal amounts of butter to flour

To make the puff pastry:

Sift the flour.

Cut the butter into small pieces.

Add half the fat to the flour with a pinch of salt and cold water to make a dough.

Knead it quickly and roll until approximately ¾ inch (19 mm) thick.

Add the remaining butter.

Fold and roll again, dusting each time with a little flour.

To make the filling:

Put the apricots and the sugar in a saucepan.

Cook gently until the apricots are reduced to a pulp.

Leave to cool.

When cold, beat in the egg yolks and the cream.

Whisk the egg whites until stiff and fold into the mixture.

Roll out ⅔ of the pastry and line a pie dish with it.

Turn the apricot mixture into the pastry case.

Roll out the remaining pastry and cover the filling, moistening the edges to seal.

Brush the pastry with milk to glaze.

Bake for 10 minutes in a very hot oven.

Reduce the temperature and continue cooking for a further 10 minutes.

Oven: 450°F/230°C Gas Mark 8
Reduce to: 350°F/180°C Gas Mark 4

BLACKBERRY PIE

Pies have been popular in England since the Middle Ages. This recipe dates from the 19th century.

For the pastry:
10 oz (275 g) flour
A pinch of salt
5 oz (150 g) butter
A little water to mix

For the filling:
2 cooking apples
1½ lbs (675 g) blackberries
4 oz (100 g) caster sugar
A little milk to glaze

To make the pastry:

Sift the flour and salt.

Rub in the butter until the mixture resembles breadcrumbs.

Add enough cold water to make a soft dough.

Leave to rest for 30 minutes.

Roll out ⅔ of the dough and line a 2 pint (1.15 litres/ 5 cups) pie dish.

To make the filling:

Peel, core and slice the apples.

Put the apple slices into a saucepan and stew gently for about 15 minutes, adding a little water if necessary.

Wash the blackberries and put into the pastry-lined pie dish.

Sprinkle with the sugar.

Pour the stewed apple over.

Roll out the remaining pastry and place over the filling, moistening the edges to seal securely.

Brush with a little milk to glaze.

Sprinkle with a little caster sugar.

Bake for 10 minutes in a fairly hot oven.

Reduce the temperature and continue cooking for 30 minutes.

Serve hot or cold with cream.

Oven: 400°F/200°C Gas Mark 6
Reduce to: 325°F/160°C Gas Mark 3

STRAWBERRY AND PORTYNGGALE SHORTCAKE

Serves 4-6

In the works of Shakespeare oranges are referred to as 'Portynggales' after oranges from Portugal.

For the shortcake base:
8 oz (225 g) flour
A pinch of salt
5 oz (150 g) butter
4 oz (100 g) caster sugar
Grated rind and juice of 1 orange

For the topping:
½ oz (15 g) gelatine
3 tablespoons orange liqueur
2 tablespoons honey
¼ pint (150 ml/ ⅔ cup) water
1 lb (450 g) strawberries
¼ pint (150 ml/ ⅔ cup) double cream

To make the shortcake:

Sift the flour and salt.

Rub in the butter.

Stir in the sugar.

Add the grated rind and juice of the orange.

Knead to make a soft dough.

Chill for 30 minutes.

Roll out and line an 8 inch (20 cm) flan ring or sandwich tin.

Bake for 20 minutes.

To make the topping:

Dissolve the gelatine in the water.

Add 2 tablespoons of the orange liqueur.

Stir in the honey.

Spread a little of the glaze over the baked shortcake.

Whip the cream and stir in the remaining tablespoon of orange liqueur.

Spoon or pipe the cream around the edge of the shortcake.

Wash and hull the strawberries.

Put the strawberries onto the middle of the shortcake and pour the remaining glaze over.

Chill before serving.

Oven: 350°F/180°C Gas Mark 4

APPLE DELIGHT

This rhyme comes from Newbold on Avon, near Rugby:
> 'At Michaelmas and a little before,
> Away goes the apple along with the core;
> At Christmas and a little bit arter,
> A crab in the hedge is worth looking arter.'

For the pastry:
6 oz (175 g) self-raising flour
3 oz (75 g) butter
A little water to mix

For the filling:
1 lb (450 g) cooking apples
2 oz (50 g) brown sugar
1 egg white

To make the pastry:

Sift the flour.

Rub in the butter until the mixture resembles breadcrumbs.

Add a little cold water to make a soft dough.

Leave to rest for 30 minutes.

Roll out the pastry and line a flan dish with it.

Bake blind for 20 minutes until golden brown.

To make the filling:

Peel, core and slice the apples.

Put into a saucepan with the sugar and a very little water, to prevent the bottom of the pan from burning.

Cook gently for about 15 minutes until the apples are soft.

Beat well and turn into the cooked pastry case.

Whisk the egg white until stiff and spread over the apple.

Cook in a hot oven for about 5 minutes to brown the topping.

Serve with blackcurrant jam and cream.

Oven: 425°F/220°C Gas Mark 7

RHUBARB COMPOTE   Serves 4

1 lb (450 g) rhubarb
6 oz (175 g) brown sugar
Grated rind of ½ a lemon
A pinch of ground ginger

Wash and chop the rhubarb, removing any stringy skin.

Put into a saucepan with a very little water to prevent the bottom of the pan from burning.

Stew gently for 20-30 minutes until completely soft and mushy.

Stir in the grated lemon rind and a pinch of ground ginger.

Transfer to a serving dish and sprinkle with the sugar.

Serve with cream.

RHUBARB CHARLOTTE

Serves 6

2 oz (50 g) butter
8 oz (225 g) breadcrumbs
1½ lbs (675 g) rhubarb
3 oz (75 g) sugar
1 teaspoon ground ginger
A pinch of cinnamon
A pinch of nutmeg
Grated rind and juice of 1 orange
3 tablespoons golden syrup
Juice of 1 lemon

Melt the butter in a saucepan and stir in the breadcrumbs.

Spoon some of the breadcrumbs into a greased 2 pint (1.15 litres/ 5 cups) pie dish.

Wash, trim and chop the rhubarb.

Put some of the rhubarb into the pie dish.

Mix the sugar, ginger, cinnamon, nutmeg and orange rind together.

Sprinkle some over the rhubarb in the pie dish.

Continue the layers in the order breadcrumbs, rhubarb, sugar, ending with a layer of breadcrumbs.

Heat the golden syrup, orange and lemon juice gently and pour over the ingredients in the pie dish.

Cover with greaseproof paper.

Bake in a moderately hot oven for 30 minutes.

Remove the greaseproof paper and continue cooking for 10 minutes to brown the top.

Serve with cream.

Oven: 400°F/200°C Gas Mark 6

BLACKBERRY ROLL

Serves 6

The hedgerows of Warwickshire are full of blackberries. In the autumn, children used to be sent out to pick them for this delicious pudding and for blackberry pie, curd and pickle.

8 oz (225 g) self-raising flour
A pinch of salt
2 oz (50 g) butter
¼ pint (150 ml/ ⅔ cup) milk
1½ lbs (675 g) blackberries
2 oz (50 g) caster sugar
A pinch of cinnamon

Sift the flour and salt.

Rub in the butter.

Stir in enough milk to make a soft dough.

Knead the dough and roll out to make a rectangle ½ inch (1 cm) thick.

Wash the blackberries and spread them onto the dough.

Sprinkle the sugar and cinnamon over the blackberries.

Roll up the dough and blackberries like a Swiss-roll, and moisten the edges to seal.

Place the roll with the join downwards on a greased baking sheet.

Brush with a little milk and bake in a moderate oven for 30 minutes.

Oven: 400°F/200°C Gas Mark 6

QUAKER'S CHOCOLATE PUDDING Serves 4

4 oz (100 g) butter
4 oz (100 g) plain chocolate
¼ pint (150 ml/ ⅔ cup) milk
4 oz (100 g) fresh breadcrumbs
3 oz (75 g) caster sugar
A few drops of vanilla essence
3 eggs

In a small saucepan melt the butter and chocolate.

Add the milk and breadcrumbs.

Stir well and cook for 10 minutes.

Leave to cool down a little.

Beat in the sugar and vanilla essence.

Separate the eggs and beat the yolks into the chocolate mixture.

Whisk the egg whites until stiff and fold them in.

Turn into a well greased 2 pint (1.15 litres/ 5 cups) pudding basin.

Cover with buttered greaseproof paper and foil and tie down with string.

Place the basin in a saucepan with enough water to come halfway up the sides.

Steam for 1 hour, topping up with water if necessary.

Serve with cream.

SPOTTED DICK

8 oz (225 g) self-raising flour
A pinch of salt
3 oz (75 g) caster sugar
3 oz (75 g) shredded suet
4 oz (100 g) currants
¼ pint (150 ml/ ⅔ cup) milk

Sift the flour and salt together.

Add the sugar, suet and currants and mix well.

Pour in enough milk to make a soft dough.

Knead lightly on a floured surface.

Turn into a greased 1½ pint (900 ml/ 3¾ cups) pudding basin.

Cover with greaseproof paper and foil and tie down with string.

Put the pudding basin into a large saucepan of boiling water.

Steam for 2 hours.

Serve with custard.

PLUM PUDDING

Serves 8-10

Plum pudding was traditionally served on various farming occasions throughout the year. One such event was the Plough Monday meal which symbolised the beginning of the farming year. It was held on the first Monday after the 12th Day (being the 6th January). It was also traditionally served after 'bean setting' (sowing), and at the Harvest Home supper later in the farming year.

3 oz (75 g) prunes
3 oz (75 g) self-raising flour
A pinch of salt
A pinch of baking powder
A pinch of grated nutmeg
A pinch of ground cinnamon
½ teaspoon mixed spice
A pinch of ground ginger
6 oz (175 g) fresh breadcrumbs
3 oz (75 g) soft brown sugar
3 oz (75 g) shredded suet
10 oz (275 g) mixed dried fruit
1 oz (25 g) chopped mixed peel
1 oz (25 g) chopped blanched almonds
1 cooking apple
Grated rind and juice of 1 orange
4 tablespoons ale
2 tablespoons rum
1 egg

Soak the prunes overnight.

Drain, remove the stones and chop the prunes.

Sift the flour, salt and baking powder together.

Add the grated nutmeg, ground cinnamon, mixed spice and ground ginger.

Add the breadcrumbs, sugar and suet.

Add the dried fruit, mixed peel and almonds.

Peel, core and grate the apple and add to the mixture.

Add the grated rind and juice of the orange, the ale, rum and the egg.

Mix the ingredients well to form a soft, dropping consistency, adding more rum if necessary.

Spoon the mixture into greased 2 lb (1 kg) pudding basin.

Cover with greaseproof paper and then foil or a pudding cloth, making a pleat in the centre to allow the pudding to rise, and tie down securely with string.

Place the pudding basin in a saucepan with enough boiling water to come half way up the sides.

Steam for 4 to 4½ hours, topping up with water if necessary.

The pudding will keep for several months if stored in a cool dry place.

Steam for a further 1½-2 hours from cold before serving.

COMPOTE OF PRUNES
AND APRICOTS

Serves 6

8 oz (225 g) dried prunes
8 oz (225 g) dried apricots
¼ pint (150 ml/ ⅔ cup) sweet sherry
2 oz (50 g) brown sugar
1 stick of cinnamon
Rind and juice of 2 oranges
½ pint (300 ml/ 1¼ cups) water

Soak the prunes and apricots in water overnight.

Drain.

Cut off the outer rind of the orange and cut it into thin strips.

Put the sherry, sugar, cinnamon and orange rind into a saucepan.

Add the prunes and apricots.

Bring to the boil and simmer for 15-20 minutes or until the prunes and apricots are tender.

Remove the cinnamon stick.

Add the orange juice and serve warm or cold with cream.

WARWICK PUDDING

2 oz (50 g) chopped crystallized ginger
1 oz (25 g) gelatine
A little milk
2 egg yolks
3 oz (75 g) caster sugar
¾ pint (450 ml/ 2 cups) single cream
¼ pint (150 ml/ ⅔ cup) rum
4 egg whites

Butter a 2 pint (1.15 litres/ 5 cups) mould.

Sprinkle the inside of the mould with the crystallized ginger.

Dissolve the gelatine in a little milk.

Beat the egg yolks with the sugar in a double boiler until it thickens.

Stir in the cream, rum and dissolved gelatine.

Beat the egg whites until stiff and fold into the mixture.

Spoon into the mould and leave in the refrigerator to set.

Turn out to serve.

STRATFORD SYLLABUB

Serves 4

½ pint (300 ml/ 1¼ cups) double cream
¼ pint (150 ml/ ⅔ cup) white wine
Grated rind and juice of 1 lemon
4 tablespoons brandy
3 oz (75 g) caster sugar
A little grated nutmeg

Mix the lemon rind, lemon juice, wine and brandy together in a bowl and leave for a few hours.

Transfer the liquid to a saucepan and add the sugar.

Heat gently until the sugar has dissolved.

Leave to cool.

Whisk the cream until stiff and stir into the liquid.

Whisk again until the mixture stands in soft peaks.

Turn into glasses and sprinkle with a little grated nutmeg.

Serve chilled.

PUCK'S POTION

Serves 4

This light summer pudding is named after the character from Shakespeare's play *A Midsummer Night's Dream*.

½ oz (15 g) gelatine
4 tablespoons golden syrup
4 eggs
Grated rind and juice of 1 lemon
¾ pint (450 ml/ 2 cups) whipping cream

Melt the gelatine in a little hot water.

Add 3 tablespoons of the golden syrup.

Separate the eggs.

Whisk the egg whites until stiff.

Fold the egg whites into the gelatine and syrup mixture.

Turn into a greased soufflé dish and chill.

Turn out of the mould and serve with the sauce.

To make the sauce:
Beat the eggs yolks until creamy.

Mix in the remaining tablespoon of golden syrup, the grated rind and lemon juice.

Whip the cream and stir into the egg mixture.

Chill until needed.

NEGRITA

This is a 19th century recipe for a rich chocolate mousse.

4 oz (100 g) bitter chocolate
3 eggs
A pinch of salt
4 tablespoons brandy
¼ pint (150 ml/ ⅔ cup) double cream, whipped

Melt the chocolate in the top of a double boiler or in a basin in a saucepan of boiling water.

Separate the eggs and add the yolks to the melted chocolate.

Add a pinch of salt and whisk until the mixture is very thick.

Stir in the brandy and leave to cool.

Whisk the egg whites until stiff but not dry-looking.

Fold them into the chocolate mixture.

Turn into individual glasses.

Chill and serve topped with the whipped cream.

HEDGEHOG TIPSY CAKE

Serves 8

Dishes that look like animals have been made since the Middle Ages. In the earliest recipes for this dish the hedgehogs were made of a marzipan-like paste moulded to look like a hedgehog and stuck all over with almonds then surrounded by jelly or cream.

1 sponge cake 8 inches (20 cm) in diameter
½ pint (300 ml/ 1¼ cups) sweet sherry
4 tablespoons apricot jam
1 oz (25 g) dark chocolate
4 oz (100 g) flaked almonds
3 raisins
½ pint (300 ml/ 1¼ cups) double cream
Juice of 1 orange
1 oz (25 g) caster sugar
3 tablespoons redcurrant jelly

Cut the sponge cake into an oval shape to look like a hedgehog and place on a serving dish.

Pour the sherry onto the cake and leave for 1 hour.

Spread the cake with apricot jam.

Grate the chocolate and sprinkle all over.

Stick the almonds into the cake facing backwards to resemble the spines of a hedgehog.

Use the raisins for eyes and a nose.

Whip the cream until thick.

Add the orange juice and the sugar.

Pipe or spoon the cream around the hedgehog.

Spoon the redcurrant jelly in front of the hedgehog's nose as though the animal was eating it!

SEEDE CAKE

8 oz (225 g) flour
A pinch of salt
1 teaspoon baking powder
4 oz (100 g) butter
4 oz (100 g) brown sugar
3 eggs
2 teaspoons caraway seeds
3 tablespoons milk

Sift the flour, salt and baking powder together.

Cream the butter and sugar until soft and fluffy.

Gradually beat in the eggs.

Fold in the flour and caraway seeds.

Add enough milk to make a soft, dropping consistency.

Put the mixture into a greased and lined 7 inch (18 cm) cake tin.

Bake in a moderate oven for 1 hour.

Take out of the oven but leave in the tin for 5 minutes before turning out onto a wire rack to cool.

Oven: 350°F/180°C Gas Mark 4

DOUGH CAKE

1 lb (450 g) flour
A pinch of salt
A pinch of ground cinnamon
A pinch of grated nutmeg
4 oz (100 g) butter
8 oz (225 g) raisins
2 oz (50 g) candied peel
½ pint (300 ml/ 1¼ cups) milk
½ oz (15 g) fresh yeast
4 oz (100 g) caster sugar

Sift the flour, salt, cinnamon and nutmeg.

Rub in the butter.

Chop the raisins and candied peel and add to the mixture.

Warm the milk to a hand-hot temperature.

Crumble in the yeast and add 1 tablespoon of the sugar.

Mix well and leave for 15 minutes, or until the liquid is frothy.

Pour the yeast liquid into the flour mixture with the remaining sugar.

Beat well and turn into a well greased cake tin.

Cover with a damp cloth and leave in a warm place until it has doubled in size.

Bake in a hot oven for 45 minutes.

Oven: 425°F/220°C Gas Mark 7

ALMOND CHEESECAKES

6 oz (175 g) butter
6 oz (175 g) caster sugar
4 egg yolks
8 oz (225 g) ground almonds
2 tablespoons orange-flower water
1 egg white

Melt the butter in the top of a double boiler or in a bowl standing in a saucepan of boiling water.

Add the sugar and stir until dissolved.

Add the egg yolks and whisk for about 15 minutes or until the mixture has thickened.

Fold in the ground almonds and the orange-flower water.

Pour the mixture into well greased patty tins.

Whisk the egg white until stiff.

Spoon the egg white over the mixture in the patty tins.

Bake for 15 minutes.

Oven: 400°F/200°C Gas Mark 6

SPONGE CAKE

This recipe has been handed down through a family from Coventry, for 130 years.

4 eggs
8 oz (225 g) sugar
A few drops of lemon essence
4 tablespoons flour
A level teaspoon baking powder

Beat the eggs, sugar and lemon essence continuously for 10 minutes.

Gradually add the flour and the baking powder.

Beat the mixture well for a further 10 minutes.

Turn into a greased 8 inch (20 cm) cake tin.

Bake for 1 hour.

Oven: 325°F/160°C Gas Mark 3

COVENTRY GODCAKES

These cakes are traditionally given to children by their Godparents at Easter and the New year. They are made in the shape of a triangle to represent the Holy Trinity.

1 lb (450 g) puff pastry
1 egg white to glaze
A little caster sugar

For the filling:
4 oz (100 g) butter
2 oz (50 g) caster sugar
12 oz (350 g) mincemeat
A pinch of mixed spice
A pinch of cinnamon
1 tablespoon rum

To make the filling:

Melt the butter.

Stir in the sugar until it has dissolved.

Add the mincemeat, mixed spice, cinnamon and rum.

Mix well.

Remove from the heat.

Roll out the pastry very thinly.

Cut into rectangles 6 inches by 8 inches (15 cm by 20 cm).

Divide the filling between the pastry rectangles, placing a portion in the middle of each.

Fold the pastry over diagonally to make a triangle, moistening the edges to seal securely.

Make 3 three slits in each triangle.

Brush with egg white and sprinkle caster sugar over each one. Bake for 15 minutes.

Oven: 400°F/200°C Gas Mark 6

JAM PUFFS

Makes 12

These are a modern day equivalent of Coventry God Cakes.

12 oz (350 g) puff pastry
1 egg white to glaze
A little caster sugar
8 oz (225 g) strawberry or raspberry jam

Roll out the pastry very thinly.

Cut into squares 4 inches by 4 inches (10 cm by 10 cm).

Put a large teaspoonful of jam into the centre of each rectangle.

Fold the squares diagonally to make triangles, moistening the edges of the pastry with the water or egg white to seal.

Brush the tops of the triangles with egg white to glaze and place onto a well greased baking sheet.

Cut three slits across the top of each triangle.

Sprinkle with caster sugar.

Bake in a hot oven for 15 minutes.

Oven: 425°F/220°C Gas Mark 7

ORANGE TEA BREAD Makes a 1 lb (450 g) loaf

Until 1940, the market square at Kineton was well-known for the sale of cheap oranges.

6 oz (175 g) self-raising flour
A pinch of salt
2 oz (50 g) butter
3 oz (75 g) caster sugar
Grated rind of 1 orange
2 tablespoons marmalade
1 egg
3 tablespoons milk
Juice of ½ an orange

Sift the flour and the salt.

Rub in the butter.

Stir in the sugar, orange rind and the marmalade.

Beat the egg with the milk and orange juice and stir into the mixture.

Turn into a well greased loaf tin.

Bake in a moderate oven for 45 minutes.

Cool on a wire rack and serve sliced, spread with butter.

Oven: 350°F/180°C Gas Mark 4

WARWICKSHIRE HONEY SCONES

Local honey is popular throughout the county.

8 oz (225 g) self-raising flour
A pinch of salt
2 oz (50 g) butter
2 tablespoons Warwickshire honey
¼ pint (150 ml/ ⅔ cup) milk

Sift the flour and the salt.

Rub in the butter.

Add the honey and enough milk to make a soft dough.

Knead the dough lightly on a floured surface.

Roll out to a thickness of about ¾ inch (2 cm).

Cut into rounds and brush with milk to glaze.

Bake in a hot oven for 10-15 minutes.

Serve with butter and honey.

Oven: 425°F/220°C Gas Mark 7

COTTAGE LOAVES

3 lbs (1.5 kg) flour
1 tablespoon salt
1 oz (25 g) lard
2 oz (50 g) fresh yeast/ or 1 oz (25 g) dried yeast
2 teaspoons sugar
1½ pint (900 ml/ 3¾ cups) warm water
1 egg

Cream the yeast with the sugar and add to the water, which should be hand-hot.

Leave for 10 minutes or until frothy.

Sift the flour and salt into a bowl and rub in the lard.

Add the yeast liquid and make a dough.

Knead for 10 minutes or until the dough is smooth and elastic.

Put in a greased bowl and cover with a clean damp cloth.

Leave in a warm place for about an hour, until the dough has doubled in size.

Knock back and knead lightly.

Divide the dough into 4 equal pieces.

Divide each piece into 2, one twice as big as the other.

Shape the larger pieces into rounds and place on greased baking trays.

Brush these pieces with salted water and top each with a smaller piece.

Press the floured handle of a wooden spoon into the centre of each loaf.

Brush each loaf with beaten egg to glaze.

Bake the loaves in a very hot oven for 5 minutes.

Reduce the temperature and continue baking for 30 minutes, until the loaves are golden brown. They should sound hollow when tapped on the base.

Oven: 450°F/230°C Gas Mark 8
Reduce to: 400°F/200°C Gas Mark 6

GINGERBREAD

1 lb (450 g) flour
6 oz (175 g) sugar
8 oz (225 g) treacle
1 oz (25 g) ground ginger
8 oz (225 g) butter
3 eggs

Mix the flour and the sugar together.

Melt the butter in a saucepan, add the treacle and the ginger and then stir the mixture into the flour and sugar.

Beat in the eggs.

Turn into a large greased loaf tin.

Bake for 1½ hours.

Oven: 300°F/150°C Gas Mark 2

DATE BREAD

Makes 2 loaves

1 lb (450 g) dried dates
½ pint (300 ml/ 1¼ cups) water
1 heaped teaspoonful of bicarbonate of soda
2 oz (50 g) butter
1 lb (450 g) flour
4 oz (100 g) brown sugar
3 eggs

Stone and chop the dates.

Boil the water and dissolve the bicarbonate of soda in it.

Pour the water over the dates.

Leave to cool.

Rub the butter into the flour.

Add the sugar.

Beat the eggs and add to the mixture.

Add the dates and water and mix well.

Knead the dough lightly.

Divide the mixture into two and shape each piece into a loaf to fit into two well greased 1 lb (450 g) loaf tins.

Bake in a moderate oven for 1½ hours.

Oven: 350°F/180°C Gas Mark 4

FRUMENTY

Frumenty was always served on Mothering Sunday. While the mother of the household was preparing the traditional meal of Stuffed Chine, her children brought her frumenty which the father of the household had laced with rum or brandy before it was served.

8 oz (225 g) cracked wheat or bulgar wheat
1 pint (600 ml/ 2½ cups) water
1 pint (600 ml/ 2½ cups) milk
8 oz (225 g) raisins
3 tablespoons honey
A pinch of grated nutmeg
A pinch of ground cinnamon
2 tablespoons rum or brandy

Wash the wheat.

Boil it in water for about 20 minutes.

Add the milk, raisins, honey, nutmeg and cinnamon.

Cook for 30 minutes over a low heat until the mixture is thick and creamy.

Add the rum or brandy and serve hot with cream.

MARROW CREAM

2 lbs (1 kg) marrow
1 lb (450 g) sugar
4 oz (100 g) butter
Grated rind and juice of 2 lemons

Peel the marrow, split in half lengthways and scoop out the seeds.

Put into a saucepan and cover with water.

Bring to the boil and simmer until the flesh is very soft.

Drain and beat to a pulp with a wooden spoon.

Return to the saucepan without the water.

Add the sugar, butter and grated rind and juice of the lemons.

Bring to the boil and simmer for about 30 minutes.

Pour into warm jars and cover with circles of greaseproof paper.

Seal tightly and store in a cool, dry place.

Use as you would lemon cheese for fillings and for spreading on toast or bread.

APPLE CHUTNEY

Makes about 3lbs

This is a very old recipe. It makes an excellent accompaniment for cold meat and meat pies.

3 lbs (1.5 kg) cooking apples
1 pint (600 ml/ 2½ cups) white wine vinegar
8 oz (225 g) sultanas
3 teaspoons salt
1 teaspoon ground ginger
2 teaspoons curry powder
½ teaspoon cayenne pepper
A few chopped shallots
12 oz (350 g) soft brown sugar

Peel, core and chop the apples.

Put the apples into a large saucepan with the vinegar, sultanas, salt, ginger, curry powder, cayenne pepper, and the chopped shallots.

Bring to the boil and simmer gently for 30 minutes.

Stir in the sugar and continue cooking gently for about 30 minutes or until the chutney is thick.

Pour into clean, dry jars up to the brim.

Cover while hot and store in a cool, dry, dark place.

This chutney is best kept for 3 months before use.

DATE JAM

Makes about 6 lbs (2.75 kg)

3 lbs (1.5 kg) dates
3 lbs (1.5 kg) carrots
3 lbs (1.5 kg) sugar
1½ pints (900 ml/ 3¾ cups) water

Stone and chop the dates.

Scrape and chop the carrots.

Put the dates and carrots into a preserving pan with the sugar and water.

Bring to the boil and boil rapidly for about 20 minutes until setting point is reached.

To test for setting point put a teaspoon of the mixture onto a cold saucer. If the mixture solidifies and wrinkles as it cools, setting point has been reached.

Pour into warm, sterilised jars and cover with greaseproof circles.

Seal tightly and store in a cool, dry place.

MINCEMEAT

3 lbs (1.5 kg) mixed dried fruit
8 oz (225 g) mixed peel
2½ lbs (1.25 kg) cooking apples
1 lb (450 g) shredded suet
8 oz (225 g) caster sugar
Grated rind and juice of 2 lemons
1 teaspoon grated nutmeg
12 oz (350 g) jam (raspberry, strawberry or
  blackcurrant)
2 tablespoons brandy

Mince the mixed dried fruit and the peel.

Peel, core and mince or grate the apples.

Mix the dried fruit, peel, apples and shredded suet together.

Stir in the sugar, lemon rind and juice, nutmeg and jam.

Add the brandy.

Mix well and turn into clean jars.

Cover with circles of greaseproof paper.

Seal tightly and store until needed in a cool, dry place.

LEMON CURD

Grated rind and juice of 3 lemons
8 oz (225 g) caster sugar
4 eggs
4 oz (100 g) unsalted butter

Mix the lemon rind and the sugar together.

Beat the eggs well and gradually add the lemon juice.

Pour the eggs and juice over the rind and sugar.

Turn into a basin in a saucepan of boiling water or into the top of a double boiler.

Add the butter and cook gently for about 20 minutes, until the butter has melted and the mixture is thick.

Pour the curd into warm jars, cover with a circle of greaseproof paper and seal.

Store in a cool place.

This curd will not keep more than a few weeks.

BLACKBERRY CURD

1 lb (450 g) blackberries
2 cooking apples
Grated rind and juice of 1 lemon
8 oz (225 g) caster sugar
4 oz (100 g) butter
4 eggs

Wash the blackberries.

Peel, core and chop the apples.

Put the blackberries and apples in a saucepan and cook gently for about 15 minutes until soft.

Rub through a fine sieve to remove the pips.

Put the pulp into the top of a double saucepan.

Add the lemon rind and juice, sugar and butter.

Beat the eggs and add to the mixture.

Cook for 30 minutes until it thickens, stirring frequently.

Pour into warm, sterilised jars or pots and cover with circles of greaseproof paper.

Seal when cold and store in a cool, dry place.

Once opened this curd will keep for a few weeks in a refrigerator.

Serve with scones, bread or hot muffins.

PICKLED BLACKBERRIES

3 lbs (1.5 kg) blackberries
½ pint (300 ml/ 1¼ cups) white wine vinegar
1 lb (450 g) sugar

Wash the blackberries.

Put the vinegar and sugar into a saucepan and heat gently.

Bring to the boil and simmer for a few minutes.

Add the blackberries and simmer for 5 minutes or until the blackberries are soft.

Remove the fruit and put into clean, dry, warm jars.

Bring the vinegar and sugar back to the boil and continue to boil rapidly until a thick syrup has formed.

Pour the syrup over the blackberries in the jars.

Seal tightly and store for a few weeks before using.

PICKLED ONIONS

2 lbs (1 kg) small pickling or silver-skin onions
2 oz (50 g) salt
2 pints (1.15 litres/ 5 cups) white wine vinegar
2 oz (50 g) mixed pickling spices
4 oz (100 g) sugar
2-3 sprigs of fresh tarragon

Top and tail the pickling onions.

Put them in bowl and pour boiling water over them.

Leave for 30 seconds.

Drain and cover with cold water.

Remove the skins under water.

Drain and sprinkle with the salt.

Cover with a clean cloth and leave over night.

Rinse and drain.

Pack into clean, dry jars.

Put a sprig of the tarragon into each jar.

Put the vinegar, mixed pickling spices (tied in a a muslin bag) and sugar in a saucepan.

Bring to the boil and simmer for 5 minutes.

Remove the spices.

Pour the vinegar into the jars to cover the onions.

Seal the jars and store for 3 weeks before using.

LEAMINGTON SAUCE

½ **pint (300 ml/ 1¼ cups) white wine vinegar**
4 **tablespoons walnut pickle or walnut ketchup**
3 **tablespoons soy sauce**
2 **tablespoons port wine**
1 **clove of garlic**
½ **teaspoon cayenne pepper**

Mix the vinegar, walnut pickle, soy sauce, port, garlic clove and cayenne pepper together.

Pour into a bottle or jar, seal and store for 3 weeks.

Strain and remove the garlic clove.

Serve with cold meat or fish.

TARRAGON VINEGAR

In the Middle Ages, vinegar was used as a preservative for vegetables and herbs. The flavoured vinegars were used in sauces, and now make good bases for salad dressings. Tarragon vinegar can be used in Tartare and Hollandaise sauce. Screw-top bottles are most suitable for storing herb vinegars.

3 oz (75 g) freshly picked tarragon
1 pint (600 ml/ 2½ cups) white wine vinegar

Reserve one or two sprigs of tarragon for decoration.

Bruise the remaining tarragon with a wooden spoon (to help bring out the flavour).

Put the bruised tarragon into a jar.

Put the vinegar into a saucepan and bring to the boil.

Pour the vinegar over the tarragon in the jar.

Seal tightly and leave in a cool, dry place for 2-3 weeks.

Strain the vinegar through muslin.

Put a sprig or two of fresh tarragon into a screw top bottle.

Pour the strained vinegar into the bottle.

Seal and store until needed.

PARSNIP WINE

3 lbs (1.5 kg) parnips
8 pints (4.5 litres) water
3 lbs (1.5 kg) sugar
1 tablespoon fresh yeast

Cut the parsnips into slices.

Boil the slices in the water until soft.

Take out the parsnips, pulp them and return to the liquid.

Add the sugar.

Boil the liquid for 30 minutes.

Leave to cool to a hand-hot temperature.

Add the yeast and leave to ferment for 1 week.

Strain the liquid and pour into bottles or jars.

Store for 6 months to a year — this wine improves with age.

WHITE ELDER WINE

3 lbs (1.5 kg) white elderberries
8 pints (4.5 litres) water
3 lbs (1.5 kg) sugar
1 lb (450 g) raisins
½ oz (15 g) citric acid
3 tablespoons wine yeast
Yeast nutrient

Remove the stalks from the elderberries.

Mince the raisins.

Boil the elderberries and raisins in the water for 30 minutes.

Strain through a sieve.

Allow the liquid to cool to a hand-hot temperature and add the yeast, yeast nutrient and citric acid.

Cover and leave in a warm place for three days, stirring daily.

Put the sugar in a bowl.

Strain the fermenting wine onto the sugar.

Pour this into stone jars or dark glass bottles.

Do not fill completely.

When the fermenting has subsided, top up the bottles or jars with cold boiled water and fit a fermentation lock.

Leave until the fermentation has finished and then siphon off into clean, dark bottles, keeping them in a dark place for 6 months.

APPLE BEER

2 lbs (1 kg) apples
Juice of ½ lemon
8 pints (4.5 litres) water
8 oz (225 g) warmed sugar
1 oz (25 g) grated root ginger
1 stick of cinnamon
½ teaspoon cloves

Wash the apples.

Grate them into the water with the lemon juice.

Cover with a cloth and leave for 7 days, stirring every day.

Strain the liquid and add the warmed sugar, grated ginger, cinnamon and cloves.

Leave overnight.

Strain and pour into bottles.

Cork lightly and leave for 1 week before drinking.

OATMEAL DRINK

This non-alcoholic and refreshing drink was popular with farm workers during the hot summer days out in the fields.

4 oz (100 g) oatmeal
12 oz (350 g) sugar
Grated rind of 1 orange
Grated rind of 2 lemons
8 pints (4.5 litres) water

Mix the oatmeal, sugar, orange and lemon rind.

Add a little of the water.

Bring to the boil and simmer for a few minutes, stirring to dissolve the sugar.

Add the rest of the water but do not re-heat.

Stir the drink and leave to cool.

Strain and serve.

THE COUNTRY RECIPE SERIES

Available now @ £1.95 each

Cambridgeshire
Cornwall
Cumberland & Westmorland
Devon
Dorset
Hampshire
Kent
Lancashire
Leicestershire
Norfolk
Oxfordshire
Somerset
Suffolk
Sussex
Warwickshire
Yorkshire

All these books are available at your local bookshop or newsagent, or can be ordered direct from the publisher. Just tick the titles you require and fill in the form below. Prices and availability subject to change without notice.

Ravette Books Limited, 3 Glenside Estate, Star Road, Partridge Green, Horsham, West Sussex RH13 8RA.

Please send a cheque or postal order, and allow the following for postage and packing. UK 25p for one book and 10p for each additional book ordered.

Name...

Address...

....

....